100 ACTION SONGS!
FOR SCHOOL KIDS

The words to these songs may be reproduced onto overhead transparencies, posters, or written on the chalkboard. We want your children's hands to be free so kids can enjoy these action songs together.

Be sure to go over each song a couple of times before you use it so that you can fit the words and tune together smoothly. Sometimes we've used symbols and sometimes we spell the words strangely to help you fit the words to the tune (for example, bri~ight). An accent mark (´) indicates which syllable to emphasize; this symbol (~) means to stretch the word; and a hyphen (-) between two words means to sing those words on the same beat. When words are repeated, repeat the actions as well. Please adapt the words and actions any way you wish.

We wish to thank these people for special help in making this little book possible:

Charlene Hiebert
Jon Kobel
Rick Thompson
Lorraine and Wes Triggs
Linda Washington

100 ACTION SONGS FOR SCHOOL KIDS

© 1989 by David C. Cook Publishing Co.

Published by David C. Cook Publishing Co.
850 N. Grove Ave., Elgin, IL 60120
Cable address: DCCOOK

Designed by Christopher Patchel and Dawn Lauck

Printed in the United States of America.

ISBN 1-555513-137-9

Contents

Songs about Jesus and God

1 Use the tune, *Michael, Row the Boat Ashore*, to help children thank God for what He's done for them.

For the love You freely give,
  Cross hands over heart; extend arms outward
Thank You, God.
  Raise arms and look up
For the world in which we live,
  Make circle with arms above head
Thank You, God.
For our parents wise and tall,
  Point to head and then stretch arm high
Thank You, God.
For good things You give us all,
  Sweep both arms forward and out
Thank You, God.

2 Sing these words, to the familiar tune *Battle Hymn of the Republic*, about what the Lord has done.

Sometimes I pause to think of what the Lord has done for me;
  March in place
How He keeps my feet from slipping and He watches over me.
Each time when I am lonely, He responds so tenderly.
  Sing slowly, looking sad; stroke left hand with right
He died for you and me.
  March in place
Refrain:
Jesus, Lord forevermo~ore!
  March in rhythm, swinging arms
Jesus, Lord forevermo~ore!
Jesus, Lord forevermo~ore!
He died for you and me.

3 Sing these worshipful words to *Fairest Lord Jesus.* Sing gently, swaying from side to side.

I love the Lord my God.
He calls me to His side.
When troubles rise, He is always near.
He tells me, when I pray,
He'll guide me everyday.
In Him I know I can abide.

4 This action song to the tune, *Buffalo Gals*, talks about Jesus' life on earth.

Jesus helped in the carpenter shop,
   Pretend to hammer or use other tools
The carpenter shop,
The carpenter shop.
As He worked He grew wise and tall.
   Squat down, then stretch tall, pointing to head
He loved His Father, God.
   Reach arms overhead

He talked with others about God's love,
   Sweep arm outward; then point up
About God's love,
About God's love.
And some fishermen answered His call
   Cup hands around mouth
To tell of His Father's love.
   Extend both arms outward

5 Sing this action rhyme to the fun melody of *This Old Man.*

I will trust God to help
   Clap hands
When things don't go right for me.
   Shuffle feet in rhythm
If I keep on trying every single day,
   Slap thighs on each syllable
Things will turn out right—you'll see!
   Snap fingers; then say "Yeah!"

6 This simple action rhyme praises God for His creation. Sing it to the tune, *Down in the Valley*.

Everything God made was very good.
   Spread arms wide
He made the twinkly stars and bright sun.
   Wiggle fingers in air; then touch fingertips overhead
He made the plants and big bears that run.
   Wave arms like branches; then run in place
Everything God made was very good.

7 Sing this rhyme about the seasons God has made to the tune *Auld Lang Syne*. Challenge children to come up with actions that depict each season. At the end of the last verse have the children jump up and cheer for God.

In SPRING I saw an open field
Where black-eyed Susans grew
And dandelions and daisies waved,
And purple clover, too.

They nodded in the SUMMER breeze,
And in their lovely way,
They asked some friendly butterflies
To stop awhile and play.

With FALL there came the cold north wind.
It blew and blew and blew.
And soon the soft, bright flowers were gone,
And autumn colors, too.

The WINTER snow fell soft and deep,
It covered all the ground
But when the sun began to shine
We knew that SPRING was 'round.

God sends the seasons every year
   Sweep right hand outward, then left
He never misses one.
   Extend both arms outward
And so let's thank Him for them all,
   Raise arms upward
So full of outdoor fun.

8 Use *This Old Man* as the tune for this action rhyme about Jesus' power.

All the things that I need,
Sweep arms outward
Every minute, every hour,
Tap wrist as if pointing to watch
I'll ask Jesus Christ to give to me—
Point up; then to self
'Cause I know He's got the power!
Squat down; then jump up on "power"

9 This rhyme, to the tune of *Fairest Lord Jesus,* helps children understand that God cares for all He's made.

The wind blows nice and warm.
Sway left and right with arms overhead
The sun shines very bright.
Make a circle with arms overhead
The birds build nests high up in the trees.
Cup hands to form nest
I see the flowers grow
Put wrists together with palms open
And hear the bumblebee.
Wiggle fingers next to ears
I know God cares for all He's made.
Spread arms wide.

10 *America the Beautiful* is the tune for these words that teach children to thank God for everything.

For grown-ups who can help us grow,
 Reach high
For apples on the tree,
 Make a ball with fingertips
For water I can drink each day,
 Make a cup with your hand and pretend to drink
For eyes, nose, feet, and knees,
 Point to these parts of the body
Give thanks to God for everything!
 Join arms with persons beside you; slowly sway
He's given these to me.
Give thanks to God for everything!
He's given these to me.

11 This rhyme about God's love and care can be sung to the tune, *Polly Wolly Doodle*.

Oh, the flowers bloom in colors bright.
 Wrists together, palms open
The birds fly high and free.
 Flap arms like a bird
I know God cares for all these things.
 Spread arms wide
I feel His love for me.
 Hug self

12 This action song of praise is to the tune, *Michael, Row the Boat Ashore*. Every time children say the word *hosanna*, indicated by (*), have them do these motions: kneel on right knee with arms outstretched; then stand and raise arms overhead.

Jesus, You know we love You. Hosanna!
Point up; cross hands over heart; then (*)
We can show You it is true. Hosanna!
Stand with feet apart, hands on hips; then (*)
We can show You with a shout. Hosanna!
We will shout to You in praise. Hosanna!
Shout the last hosanna in rhythm (*)

Jesus, You know we love You. Hosanna!
We can show You it is true. Hosanna!
We can show You with our hands. Hosanna!
Hold hands out with fingers spread; then (*)
Now, without singing, clap seven times in rhythm; then sing—**Hosanna!** (*)

13 This action rhyme, to the tune of *I'm a Little Teapot*, teaches that God forgives.

When I do~oo bad first I feel sad.
Look mad, then look sad
But God forgives me; then I'm glad.
Point up, then clap and smile

14

Sing the words for this action rhyme to the tune, *Down By the Station.*

I have a secret that I'll never whisper.
 Point to self; then put finger over mouth, shake head
I have a secret that I'll never shout.
 Point to self; cup hands around mouth, shaking head
Jesus is near us. He sees us and hears us.
 Point up, cross hands over heart; shade eyes and cup hand behind ear
Ooops! I let the secret out.
 Look surprised and sweep both arms outward

But it doesn't matter that I just now told you.
 Stand with hands on hips
It doesn't matter that I did say,
"Jesus is near us. He sees us and hears us."
For He wanted you to know anyway.
 Point up, then out, then to your head

15

Old MacDonald is the tune for this rhyme that helps kids give thanks to God.

The morning sun that wakes me up,
 Make circle with arms overhead
The new leaves on the trees,
 Move arms and fingers like tree branches
The creepy caterpillar and
 Wiggle arms like a caterpillar
The buzzing bumblebees,
 "Flap" fingers rapidly near face like a bumblebee
Arms that grow and hands that clap,
 Slowly stretch both arms; then clap once
Head and toes and fingers' snap,
 Touch head and toes; then snap fingers
Thank You God for all of these.
 Slap thighs in rhythm
Thank You, thank You, God!
 Clap in rhythm

16 The Christmas carol, *O Come, All Ye Faithful*, is a good melody for this rhyme about God's care.

O, my God is with me when I'm here or there,
  Point up; cross hands on chest; point down, then out
And He always helps me know what's right to do.
  Point up; then point to head
God loves me so much that He gives me care.
  Hug self; then point up and smile
So I'll say, "Thank You, God."
  Point to self; then to mouth; then up
So I'll say, "Thank You, God."
So I'll say, "Thank You, God. And I do love You, too!"
  Point to self; then to mouth; then up; hug self

17 Let kids act like different animals as they sing this to *Jingle Bells.* Encourage them to think of actions that emphasize what the words are saying, such as stretching tall when singing the words "extra tall."

Some animals have spots
And some are very small;
Some have thick and furry skin,
And some are extra tall.
Some animals will bark
While others like to moo.
Some will make the strangest sounds
To say, "How do you do?"

Refrain:
Some animals are wild
And some live in the zoo.
Some are pets that stay at home
And live right there with yoo~ou.
God made all the animals
That walk and hop and run.
Though all of them are different,
He cares for everyone.

18 These words, to the tune of *America the Beautiful*, talk about all that God has created.

I like to think how nice it is
God made a place for trees;
   Wave arms overhead like blowing trees
With bright red fruit and leaves of green
That flutter in the breeze.
   Wiggle fingers like fluttering leaves
Refrain:
I like to think how nice it is
God made these things to see.
   Sweep right arm from left to right
He filled the earth with lovely things.
But saved a place for me.
   Point to self

19 *Pop! Goes the Weasel* is the tune for this rhyme. Don't forget to practice the song ahead of time.

Everything that grows begins
   Crouch down as small as possible
From something very small—
A tree, a flower, a pumpkin, too—
God planned for all.
   Jump up quickly

20 Use the *Doxology* to sing this action rhyme to help children worship God.

God made the sun that shines so bright
   Make circle with arms overhead
And stars that twinkle in the night.
   Raise hands and wiggle fingers
He'll always be with me, I know
   Point up; then put hand over heart
Because the Bible tells me so.
   Hold hands like a book.

21 Sing these words about the way God cares for us to the tune, *Hush, Little Baby.*

God gives us food we need each day.
　　Rub stomach
He gives us homes and family.
　　Put fingers together overhead for a roof
He gives us all we need to live
　　Stretch arms wide
God cares for you and you and me!
　　Point to others, then to self

22 As children sing these words to the tune, *This Land Is Your Land*, have them sway slowly left to right, clapping on the beat.

God shows that Hé cares by giving tó me
My home and fó~od and family. . .
All that I née~eed and some to shá~are
With other people everywhére.

23 The commercial jingle *I Am Stuck on Band-aids* is the tune for this action rhyme.

I will stick with Jesus
　　"Stick" right hand to left hand
'Cause Jesus sticks with me.
　　Pretend to *try* to pull hands apart
I will stick with Jesus
'Cause Jesus sticks with me,
'Cause He'll never, never leave me,
　　Shake head "no"
I want the world to see
　　Shade eyes with hands
I will stick with Jesus
'Cause Jesus sticks with me.

Scripture Songs

24 Sing these words, based on John 14:6, to the tune, *If You're Happy.* Here are the actions for this song: when children sing *the way*, have them slap their thighs twice; on *the truth*, have snap their fingers twice; on *the life*, have them clap twice. After they sing the entire line, have them stomp their feet twice.

Jesus said, "I am the way, the truth, the life."
Jesus said, "I am the way, the truth, the life."
Jesus said, "I am the way;
You can trust me when you pray."
   Sing slowly
Jesus said, "I am the way, the truth, the life."

25 Sing these words of praise, based on Psalm 116:2, to the tune of *Camptown Races.*

I love the Lord; He heard my cry.
   Left hand over heart, then right hand up in air
Hallelujah!
   Snap fingers on beat
He comforts me; on Him I rely.
   Hug self; then place fists together
Hallelujah, Lord!
   Snap fingers, then raise arms
Chorus:
Hallelujah, Lord!
Hallelujah, Lord!
He comforts me; on Him I rely.
Hallelujah, Lord!

26 John 15:12-14 is the basis for this rhyme sung to the tune of *Deck the Halls*.

My command is this forever
   Sway side to side
Love each other now as I love you.
   Cross arms over heart; sweep arms up and out
Greater love can no man offer.
   Sway side to side
Love each other now as I love you.
All My love you cannot measure
   Sway side to side
It's so wide, deep inside, and it's free!
   Stretch arms wide, then deep; clap after "free"
For you are my greatest treasure,
   Sway side to side
Love each other now as I love you.

27 Use these words from Romans 10:14, 15a to introduce a discussion about missions. Sing them to *Christmas is Coming*, also called *Country Gardens*. Add action by having children mimic the statue *The Thinker* or striking another quizzical pose when they sing the word "how."

How can they call on One they've not believed?
And how can they believe if they have not heard?
How can they hear if someone doesn't preach?
And how can someone preach without being sent?

28 Sing this action song, based on James 1:22, to *Are You Sleeping?*

Do be doers, do be doers
   Shake hands and pat others on the back
Of God's Word, of God's Word,
   Hold hands like a book
Not just hearers only, not just hearers only
   Cup right hand behind ear; wave left hand "no"
Of God's Word, of God's Word.
   Clap in rhythm

29 These words, based on Psalm 121:7, 8, can be sung to *Camptown Races*.

The Lord will keep you from all harm;
  Skip in a circle
He is watching.
  Stop! Shade eyes with hand
He will guard your life always
  Skip in a circle
Watching over you.
  Stop! Shade eyes with hand
Watching when you come,
  Lean forward, shading eyes
Watching when you go,
  Turn around and shade eyes
The Lord will keep you from all harm
  Skip in a circle
Now and evermore.
  Stop with hands on hips; then raise arms upward

30 This psalm of praise to God can be sung to *Auld Lang Syne*. The words are based on Psalm 146:1, 2. Challenge the children to think of actions.

Oh, praise the Lord, O my soul.
I will praise Him all my life;
I will sing praises to my God
As long as I may live.

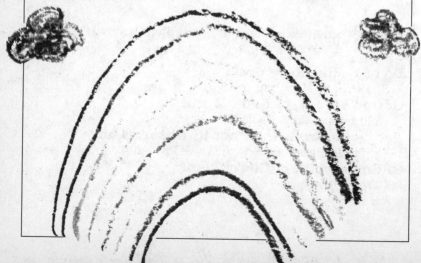

31 Sing these words, from I Chronicles 16:23, 24, to *Michael, Row the Boat Ashore.* Repeat the words and actions three times to complete the song.

Now sing to the Lord, all earth.
  Point right hand to mouth, then upward; sweep left arm outward
Sing His glory.
  Raise both arms upward
Now sing to the Lord, all earth,
  Sway left to right in rhythm
To all nations.

32 *When Johnny Comes Marching Home* is a good tune to use to sing these words from Psalm 25:1, 2. Here are some steps, called "the grapevine," that kids will enjoy doing as they sing these words: cross left foot in front of right, then step with right foot; cross left foot behind right, then step with right foot; repeat pattern. Have kids put hands on the shoulders of the kids beside them as they move sideways.

To You, O Lord, I lift my soul. We worship You.
  Grapevine right; then clap
In You I trust, O Lord, my God. We worship You.
  Grapevine left; then clap
O do not let me be put to shame, nor let my enemies win over me.
  Sway in rhythm, right to left, with arms overhead
O we worship You, our Lord and God and King.
  Grapevine right; then clap

33 John 14:6 is a familiar passage. Sing these words, based on that verse, to the tune of *Kum Ba Yah.* Each time children sing *Jesus*, have them point up. When they sing *way*, point ahead; for *truth*, place hand over heart; for *life*, sweep arms outward.

Jesus is the way, truth, and life.
Jesus is the way, truth, and life.
Jesus is the way, truth, and life.
My way, truth, and life.

34

The beautiful words of Psalm 121 have been adapted to the tune of *This Is My Father's World.*

I-lift úp my eyes to-the hills—
Shield eyes, looking upward
Where does my help co~me from?
Fold arms across chest
My help comes from th~e Lord above,
Raise arms upward
The maker of heaven and earth.
Swing arms together left to right
Refrain:
He'll not let your foot slip—
Hands on hips
He who watches you won't sleep.
Shield eyes, looking downward
Indeed, He who watches Israel
Sweep arms up and down
Will nei~ther slumber nor sleep.
Fold hands

The Lord watches over you.
Raise arms upward
The Lord is-the shade for you.
Shade head with hands
The sun will never-harm you by day,
Cup hands around face with fingers spread apart
Neith~er the moon b~y night.
Put fists together overhead
Refrain:
The Lord will keep you-from harm.
Fold arms across chest
He will watch over your life.
Sweep right arm outward
The Lord will watch as you come and go
Bend elbows, rocking arms back and forth
Both now and forev~er more.
Raise arms upward

35 Have children clap or use rhythm instruments to these words based on Psalm 9:1, 2. Sing to the tune, *This Old Man*.

I will práise You, O Lórd.
I will tell of Yóur wonders.
I will be glad and rejoice in You.
I will sing praise to Your name.

36 *Brahm's Lullaby* is a good tune to use to sing these words based on Psalm 33:1-4.

Sing-joyfully to the Lórd.
  Slowly sweep arms upward
Praise the Lord with the ha~rp;
  Pretend to strum harp
Now make music on the lyre.
Sing to Him a brand new song;
  Move hands to mouth and gesture outward
Play and shout now for joy,
For the word of the Lord
  Slowly sweep arms upward, then outward
Is right a~nd true.
He is faithful in all.

37 Here's a fun way to move in a circle as they sing words from Psalm 133:1, 2 to the tune, *Farmer in the Dell*. Have children stand in a circle with every two children standing back to back. Have them hold out their right hands and take the hand of the person facing them, walk past that person, and then grab left hands with the next person facing them. They keep going, weaving a "chain" in the circle until the song is finished.

How good and pleasant it is, (2x)
When brothers live in unity
How good and pleasant it is.

It's like precious oil, (2x)
Poured on the head and down the beard.
It's like precious oil.

Repeat the first verse.

38 Sing these words from Psalm 131:3 to the tune *Skip to My Lou*. Kids will have fun skipping in a circle as they sing.

O Israel, put your hope in the Lord. (3x)
Both now and forevermore.

39 *The Bear Went Over the Mountain* is a well-known kids tune. Use it to sing these words from Psalm 27:1. Every time children sing, "The Lord is my light and salvation," have them sweep their right arms up and out, then their left arms. When they sing, "Whom shall I fear?" have them put hands on hips.

The Lord is my light and salvation. (3x)
Whom shall I fear? (clap, clap) (3x)
The Lord is my light and salvation. (3x)
Whom shall I fear? (clap, clap)

40 Have children sing these words which have been adapted from Psalm 44:1-6 to the tune, *Fairest Lord Jesus*. Have children slowly sway to the rhythm or select some other worshipful action.

O God, our fathers
Told us all that You did
In days so very long ago.
It was not with their swords
That they conquered the land
Nor did their weapons bring vict'ry.

T'was Your right hand and arm
And the light of Your face.
For You loved them,
Yes, You loved them.
You are my God and King.
You push back enemies.
The sword does not bring victory.

Bible Story Songs

41 Use the tune, *Row, Row, Row Your Boat,* to sing this action rhyme.

Get your nets and then
  Pretend to pick up heavy nets
Throw them in the sea.
  Toss nets out to sea
Pull them in, all full of fish.
  Pull the nets back in
Then come and follow me.
  Motion others to come

42

Kids will enjoy this action rhyme to the tune, *A Hole in My Bucket.*

I'm goin' on a boat ride.
   Row with arms
But I'm not afraid!
   Shake head no and stomp feet
God is always with me.
   Point up
He's right by my side.
   Slap arm to side

The storm winds are blowing.
   Make motions with arms like blowing wind
The rain comes a falling.
   Wiggle fingers like rain
The boat begins rocking.
   Rock back and forth
We all help to row.
   Row with arms

Toss heavy things over.
   Make throwing motions
Encourage each other.
   Pat person next to you on shoulder
God said He'd be with us,
   Point up
For He loves us so.
   Hug self

We must swim to shore now.
   Make swimming motions
We are not afraid!
   Shake head no and stomp feet
God is right beside us.
   Raise arms upward
He will show us how.
   Punch the air with fist and say, "Yeah!"

43 Sing this rhyme to the chorus of *Jingle Bells.* Have children make this song a mini-play, selecting actions to use. Let them take turns being Daniel.

Dániel prayed three times a day.
He knéw that this was right.
When hé was thrown in with the lions,
God clósed their mouths up ti~ight.
Yóu can be like Dániel
When tróuble comes in sight.
Just ásk the Lord to hélp you
Make choíces that are right.

44 Use the tune, *When Johnny Comes Marching Home,* to sing the rhyme about the time Peter denied Jesus.

"Yóu're a friend of Jésus!" one by óne some people sáid.
Point as if at Peter; sweep right hand out, then left
Péter answered, "Nó!" three times, "Not I!" he shook his head.
Shake head; point to self, then hands on hips
When the róoster crowed, "Cock-a-dóodle-doo!"
Flap arms like wings
Péter cried, "Lord, I've sínned against You.
Kneel, looking sad
Please forgíve me for I wánt to follow You."
Stand, raising arms upward

45 Sing this rhyme about Moses to the tune of the familiar hymn, the *Doxology.*

Oh, Moses put his trust in God
Reach arms out, palms up
And prayed to help the people out.
Fold hands in prayer
God gave Moses the strength to lead.
Flex arm to show muscle
"Hurray!" the happy people shout.
Jump and shout happily

46

Using the melody to the **verse** of *Yankee Doodle*, have children sing this action rhyme about the conversion of Saul on the road to Damascus.

"Whát a fine young mán!" said-the Pharisees,
    Snap fingers in rhythm
As they watched Saul leáve town.
"He hátes those troublesome Chrístians,
    Slap thighs in rhythm
And he'll húnt each of them dówn."

But ón the road to Dámascus,
    Walk in place
Saul leárned his hate was si~in.
He sáw the light, so blínding bright.
    Shield eyes from bright light
His heárt the Lord did wi~in.
    Cross hands over heart, then point upward

But stíll the Christians tré~embled
    Act afraid
When sómeone mentioned Sá~ul.
To shów them he was dífferent now,
    Proudly march in place
He úsed his Greek name, Pá~ul.

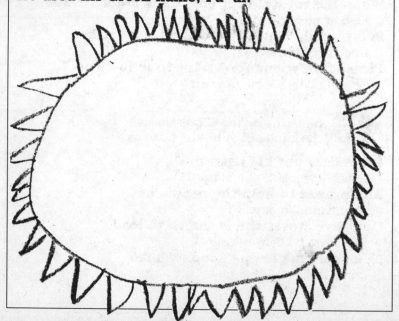

47 Sing this action rhyme about Jonah to the tune for the chorus of *Jingle Bells*.

In the fish, in the fish
　Squat down
It's sure dark in here.
　Cover eyes
Should have done just what God said,
　Point to self, nodding head
But I went my own way.
　Hang head down, looking sorry
In the fish, in the fish—
　Squat down
I'll kneel down and pray,
　Kneel to pray, but stay curled up
Because it isn't any good
　Stand with hands on hips
Unless I walk God's way.
　Walk in place, pointing upward

48 Sing this story about Sarah from the Old Testament to *Pop Goes the Weasel*.

Sárah asked Gód to gíve her a son.
　Fold hands in prayer
She wáited many yéars.
　Look sad; pretend to cry
God gáve her little báby Isaác
　Rock baby
And dríed up all her téars.
　Smile and clap in rhythm

Sometímes God tells us eé~each to wait.
　Now bend knees on each beat
He sáys, "The time's not rí~ight."
We nééd to learn to trúst in Him more
To máke the future brí~ight.

49

Sing this story about the life of Peter to *Oh, Susanna*. Let children decide how to act out the verses. When they sing the refrain, have them clap in rhythm, two claps to the left, two to the right. Sing the refrain after each verse or just once after the last verse.

Refrain:
Rejoice, people!
We need to give God praise,
Because Péter served God fáithfully
The rést of his dáys.

Verses:
Whe~en Jésus calls dear Pé~e~ter
To-a life that is néw,
The~e físherma~an fóllows Him
And leárns what to do.

One níght Peter hurts Je~e~sús
By télling some lies.
At dáwn the rooster cróws three times
And bráve Peter cries.

Now Jésus' love forgíves Peter.
And hé is so gráteful.
Peter vóws to fee~eed Jésus' sheep
And kéep them fáithful.

Peter bóldly speaks out éverywhere;
His wórds do not fáil,
Even whén King Herod cáptures him
And púts him in jáil.

But-the thíck walls in the prí~ison
Cannót make Peter stáy,
Because Gód Himself guards Pé~eter
And áll of those who pray.

50 Older kids will enjoy doing this next action rhyme as a "rap"—a talking song or reading to a rhythm. Divide children into two groups: one group can do the actions and the other group can keep the beat by clapping, snapping fingers, slapping thighs, or using rhythm instruments. All the kids should say the rap together. This mark (´) shows you when the accent or beat comes.

A lóng time agó God's péople were sád
   Make sad face; act afraid
For the kíng of Égypt was véry bád.
God sáid to the péople, "I'll máke you frée.
   Point up and dry tears
Lísten to Móses and fóllow Mé."
   Motion to come
When they cáme to the séa God knéw what to dó.
He ópened the wáters and lét them go thróugh!
   Put palms together; then spread them apart
Into the désert they wént, and thén,
God's péople sóon were unháppy agáin.
   Act sad again
"We're húngry," lóts of péople saíd.
"Wé need méat! Wé need bréad!"
   Rub stomaches; cup hands around mouth
"Gód will sénd you foód each dáy,"
The péople soón heard Móses sáy.
   Cup hands by ears
The péople heárd a whírring soúnd.
Bírds were lying áll aroúnd!
   Pretend to fly
"God sént us méat," the péople saíd.
"And ín the mórning He'll sénd us bréad."
   Look happy and excited
Ín the mórning the péople foúnd
Sómething white all óver the gróund.
   Sweep arms outward
The péople áte it. "My, how góod!
God sént us mánna fór our foód."
   Pretend to eat; point up, looking happy
God lóves His péople; that's why, you sée,
He gíves good thíngs to yóu and mé.
   Sweep arms outward then upward

51 Here's another rap to challenge older children. This rhyme is about people in Jesus' day wondering who He was. This rhyme doesn't have actions, but let children come up with creative ways of keeping the beat. Remember that the accent mark (´) indicates where the beat comes. When you see this mark (x), it means that the kids should keep the rhythm going, but they don't say anything on that beat.

The Phárisees sáid, "We're gétting pretty mád.
This Jésus does thíngs that bréak our little rúles.
He eáts with sínners; on the Sábbath He héals.
Doésn't He knów that's júst not very cóol?"

Well, Jésus sáid, "Those Phárisées
Are wáy off báse and blínd.   x´
They're pícky, they're pétty, they thínk they
     know it áll;
But they háven't got a clúe to what is ón my
     mínd.
Well, whó do théy say thát I ám?"

They sáy you're júst a cárpenter's són,
That Gód You símply can't bé.   x´
You ónly cause tróuble aróund this tówn.
We're wárning You, Jésus, You're their énemy.

Other fólks saw Jésus' déeds,
And, yés, their mínds were blówn.   x´
They sáid, "He múst be quíte a gúy.
Let's pút Him ón the thróne."   x´

Well, Jésus sáid, "Those gúys are wróng
Who wánt to máke Me Kíng.   x´
I'm télling yóu for ónce and áll
That's réally nót My thíng.   x´
Well, whó do péople say thát I ám?"

Some péople sáy You áre the gréatest.
They sáy You shóuld be rúler—   x´
A próphet whó's come báck to lífe.
Man, Yóu can't gét much cóoler!   x´

Jésus sáid, "They've gót it wróng.
We've gót to léave this pláce!"   x´
And thén He túrned and lóoked at thém.
"How dó you pléad My cáse?   x´

"Peter, whó do yóu say thát I ám?
You've sáid to Mé what óthers sáy.
I wónder whát you thínk.   x´
And Péter—'caúse he wás real bóld,
Spoke úp withoút a blínk.   x´

"I've wátched Yóu; I've tálked with Yóu.
I've séen the wórks You've dóne.   x´
There's ónly óne choice thát is ríght—
You áre the Chríst, God's Són!   x´

Songs about Family and Friends

52 Sing this fun action rhyme to *Jimmy Crack Corn*.
Have children pick a partner for this song.

I am playing with my friend.
   Skip with your partner
Fun like this should never end.
We're bouncing balls and climbing trees
   Pretend to do these fun things together.
And running races in the breeze.
Refrain:
Toe the mark and then shout, "Go!"
   Get set to start a race
Our four feet are never slow.
   Run in place
Down the walk we run with glee.
Running makes us feel so free.

53 Have children link arms and slowly sway as they sing these words to *Fairest Lord Jesus.*

Show love to your neighbors.
Give friends a helping hand.
Think loving thoughts.
Let your words be kind.
Caring for folks you know
Is the best way to show
That you love God and all mankind.

54 Using the tune for *The Wheels on the Bus,* have kids sing this and then think of things they should share with friends. The things they think of should have three syllables so they fit the rhythm of the song— new skateboard, baseball glove, cassette tape, video game.

I will share because I care,
'Cause I care, 'cause I care.
I will share because I care.
I'll share because I care.

I will share my ___ ___ ___,

___ ___ ___, ___ ___ ___.
I will share my ___ ___ ___,
I'll share because I care.

55 Use the tune to *If You're Happy and You Know It* to sing this action rhyme. If you wish, substitute some other fun action, such as jumping, for the two claps.

You're a winner when you're helpful and you're
    true. (2x)
    Raise hands overhead like a winner; then clap twice
You accomplish quite a lot
    Make a muscle with right arm
'Cause God's power is in you.
    Make a muscle with left arm
You're a winner when you're helpful and you're
    true.
    Raise hands overhead like a winner; then clap twice

56

Sing this rhyme to the tune of *Skip to My Lou*.
Use the questions as discussion starters. Challenge kids to think of their own motions as they sing.

My párents give me rules to obey.
Do Í have to follow them every day?
"Do thís, not that," adults always say.
Why am I punished for-wanting my-way?

My friénd has a problem-and it's no fun to play.
Should Í say good-bye and go my-own way?
I háve what I need and more than-my share.
What should I do to show-that-I care?

When schóol is hard and-my work's not done,
Why should I study when-I want-to-have fun?
I wánt folks to trust me and like me, too.
Hów can I show that-I'm-honest-and true?

57 This fun, winter-time action rhyme, called "Beat the Winter Blahs," is to the tune of *Kum Ba Yah*. Every time the kids sing "beat the winter blahs," have them sit down, slump in their chairs and hang their head. When they sing the next phrase, have them jump up quickly and act out what the words say. They might enjoy thinking of their own rhymes.

Beat the winter blahs. Ride a sled.
Beat the winter blahs. Stand on your head.
Beat the winter blahs. Shine your shoes.
And then, read the news.

Beat the winter blahs. Change your room.
Beat the winter blahs. Plant a bloom.
Beat the winter blahs. Sweep the rug.
And then, give Mom a hug.

Beat the winter blahs. Feed the birds.
Beat the winter blahs. Learn new words.
Beat the winter blahs. Pray for your friends.
And then, do deep knee bends.

Beat the winter blahs. Learn to knit.
Beat the winter blahs. Oil your mitt.
Beat the winter blahs. Write a letter.
And then, you'll soon feel better.

58 Sing this short action rhyme to the tune of *Down in the Valley*.

When you are wand'ring
    Shield eyes, looking all around
And can't find the way,
    With quizzical expression, point to head
Just read the Bible
    Hold hands like book
For directions each day.
    March in place

59

Sing this action rhyme, to the tune of *Deck the Halls*, about how wonderfully God made us.

Thank You for my hands to clap.
Clap in rhythm
Thank You for my arms to reach up high.
Stretch and wave arms
Thank You for my feet to run
Run in place
And jump way up almost to the sky.
Jump in place
Thank You for my nose to sniff;
Wiggle nose
Also, thank You for my eyes to see.
Circle eyes with fingers
Thank You for my ears to hear
Cup hands behind ears
All about the gifts You've given me.
Extend arms, then raise them upward

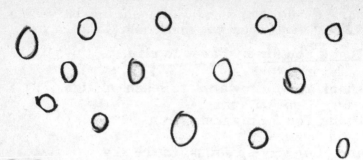

60 This rhyme, a variation on *The 12 Days of Christmas*, is called "The First Days of Winter." This familiar Christmas tune has 12 verses. Each verse adds a new line and action until the entire song is sung for verse 12. Because there isn't room in this small book to write out all the verses and repeat the actions, here are the first couple to get you started and then the last verse completely written out. The tempo for the new words on the fifth verse is very different—slow and sustained. Instead of "Five golden rings," sing "Let's go inside!"

On the first day of winter
 Stand at attention
My best friend said to me,
 Put arm around shoulder of friend next to you
"Let's sit by the crackling warm fire."
 Sit down; rub hands to warm them; relax

On the second day of winter
My best friend said to me,
"Please take a cookie.
 Pretend to eat
And let's sit by the crackling warm fire."

On the twelfth day of winter
My best friend said to me,
"How I love winter!
 Jump up and down
Try my new sled.
 Pretend to slide down a hill
We can build a snow fort.
 Pretend to build fort
Let's throw some snowballs.
 Throw pretend snowballs

Our gloves are wet.
    Shake both hands and make a face
Your nose looks red.
    Rub nose
My feet are chilly.
    Stomp feet
Let's~go~inside!
    Motion for friend to come with you
Take off your coat.
    Take off big, heavy coat
Have a cup of cocoa.
    Pretend to drink
Please take a cookie.
And let's sit by the crackling warm fire."

61
Sing this action rhyme to *Mulberry Bush.* Have children select partners and act out these words to each other.

Can you come out and play with me?
    Motion for partner to come with you
I'm as lonesome as can be.
    Look sad
I just moved here the other day.
So won't you please come out to play.
    Motion for partner to come with you

I will gladly play with you.
    Nod yes; partner jumps up and down
'Cause I am lonesome sometimes, too.
I know a lot of games to play.
So won't you visit here today?

62 Sing this action rhyme to *Polly Wolly Doodle.* Have children clap in rhythm each time they sing the verse. Then have volunteers act out each of the animals that the words talk about. Remember that this mark (´) means to accent that syllable.

Verse:

God gáve each animál a home.
Some séttle down, some chóose to roam,
Some líve on land, some ín the sea,
Some únderground, some ín a tree.

"I am glad, I am glad,
I am glad," said Furry Bear.
"I have a cave in which to sleep
In winter's cold or summer's heat."

Repeat verse
"I am glad, I am glad,
I am glad," said Hooty Owl.
"I have a home up in a tree
Where bright green leaves will shelter me."

Repeat verse
"I am glad, I am glad,
I am glad," said Finny Fish.
"I have a home down in the sea
Where all my friends will swim with me."

Repeat verse
"I am glad, I am glad,
I am glad," said Slippery Snail.
"I have a home upon my back,
So shelter's not a thing I lack."

Repeat verse
"I am glad, I am glad,
I am glad," said Miner Mole.
"I have a hole down underground
Where lots of juicy grubs are found."

63 The Sunday school song, *The Wise Man Built His House Upon a Rock*, is the tune for this rhyme.

If you would like to learn to be wise, (3x)
 Point outward, then to head
Then open up your eyes.
 Make circles around eyes with thumbs and fingers

Chorus:
Open úp your eyes and réad God's Word (3x)
 Hold hands like a book
They're the best words ever heard.
 Sweep arm outward; then cup hand behind ear

Obey God's Word and you will be wise. (3x)
 Hold hands like book, then point to head
So open up your eyes.
 Make circles around eyes with thumbs and fingers
Repeat chorus

64 Here are a couple of ways to do this rhyme to the tune, *B-I-N-G-O*: Have kids trace the letters of Jesus' name in the air as you sing them (sing the letters slowly); or, have them clap as they sing the letters.

Jesus is a friend to me.
A better friend there could not be.
J-E-S-U-S (3x)
Jesus is my best friend.

Jesus loves me this I know
For in God's Word it tells me so.
J-E-S-U-S (3x)
I'm glad that Jesus loves me.

Songs about Prayer

65 As children sing this prayer to the tune of the *Doxology,* have them sway slowly from side to side in rhythm.

Come, Lord, and hear our grateful praise.
We give to You our years and days.
Help us to give our best to You,
And to Your Word we will be true.

66 Use this action rhyme to teach children the importance of praying for missionaries. Sing it to the tune, *This Old Man.*

While you work far away
May Jésus help you every day.
The~en when I pray, I'll thi~ink of you
And thank the Lord for all you do.

67 This prayer can be sung to *God Is So Good.* Encourage children to do the actions reverently.

Lord, hear our praise. (2x)
   Slowly raise both arms
Grant us Your peace.
   Slowly lower arms, cross hands over heart
Visit us today.
   Fold hands in prayer

68

Sing this action song about prayer to the tune *This Land Is Your Land.*

When I'm in bed at-night,
  Rest head on hands
I talk to God in-prayer.
  Fold hands in prayer
I know I'll be all-right
  Hands on hips
'Cause He is always-there.
  Cross hands over heart
So when I close my-eyes,
  Cover eyes with hands
I sleep until sunrise.
  Put right arm on left; lift right hand as if sun rising
My God!—He cares for you and me.
  Point up; then out and to self

69

Let the children select the actions for this simple song to the tune *Are You Sleeping?* After kids become familiar with the words, sing this as a round.

I am praying, I am praying
For my friends, for my friends.
God wants me to do this. God wants me to do this.
He hears my prayer; He answers prayer.

70

Sing this song about prayer to to the gentle melody of *Kum Ba Yah.*

In the dárk sometimes I am scared
  Cover eyes; then look afraid
When I'm in my bed late at night.
  Rest head on hands
Then I talk to God in prayer,
  Point up, then fold hands in prayer
And-I know I'll be-all right.
  Hug self and smile

71

Use the tune to the familiar hymn, *Fairest Lord Jesus*, to sing this prayer.

Lord, I am feeling down,
Bow head, looking sad
And no one is around.
Shade eyes and look back and forth
Please, won't you lift my spirits now?
Slowly sweep hands upward
Even now as I pray,
Fold hands in prayer
Take all my cares away.
Sweep hands down and away
I want to trust you more each day.
Put fists together

72

Using the tune to *Twinkle, Twinkle Little Star*, challenge kids to fill in the blanks with things for which they'd like to thank God—things such as Troy and Sue, green and blue; or frogs and lizards, storms and blizzards.

Thank You, God, for being there.
Thank You, God, I know You care.
Thank You, God, for ___ and ___.
Thank You, God, for ___ and ___.
Thank You, God, for being there.
Thank You, God, I know You care!

Songs about Church and Sunday School

73 Sing this song about the many ways we can worship God to the tune, *Polly Wolly Doodle*. Let children select a different action for each of these verses. For example, they could clap in rhythm on the first verse, sway back and forth on the second, and swing their arms from right to left on the third verse.

When people sing their praise to You,
They're worshiping in song.
I like to listen to the sound
And also sing along.
Songs of praise, songs of praise,
Songs of praise we'll sing to You.
We worship You in many ways
And gladly give You praise.

The people pray and give You thanks.
Your love is plain to see.
You sent Your Son to die for us.
I'm glad that You love Me!
Prayers of thanks, prayers of thanks,
Prayers of thanks we give to You.
We worship You in many ways
And gladly give You praise.

And when I hear the people tell
About Your loving care.
I know You're watching over me.
I'm glad You're always there!
I will tell, I will tell,
I will tell them of Your care.
We worship You in many ways
And gladly give You praise.

74 Sing this action rhyme about missions to the fun tune *Pop Goes the Weasel*.

Our missionaries are on the go
Run in place
All around the world,
Sweep right hand outward
Helping Jesus' church to grow.
Squat down, then stretch upward
God's message they have hurled.
Point to mouth then fling arm outward

75 Use the tune, *I've Been Working on the Railroad*, to sing this action rhyme. After children become familiar with it, let them come up with more actions.

Some kids go to church because they do just what folks say.
Move around like robots
Other people go to church just to pass the time of day.
Point to wrist
Some kids think that church is boring—
Look bored
Why rise up so early in the morn?
Stretch, yawn
Some kids go to church so they can toot-toot their own horn.
Pretend to blow horn
That's not why I go, that's not why I go,
That's not why I go to chu~ur~urch.
That's not why I go, that's not why I go,
That's not why I go to church.
I go bée~cause God loves me and I love Him too~oo~oo.
I love God and He loves me—that's why I go to church
Sing~ing~
Glo~ry hallelujah! Glory hallelujah~ha~ha~ha!
Glo~ry hallelujah!~~That's why I go to church.

76 Have children snap their fingers to this lively tune, *Skip to My Lou*, and sing this rhyme that teaches them about the purpose of the offering.

A picture of Jesus or books for our room,
A mop for the janitor, maybe a broom,
A Bible for children who live far away,
My off'ring will help to buy this today.

A penny, a nickle, a quarter or dime.
The off'rings I bring help someone every time.
Sharing our money is what we should do
So others will learn the Bible is true.

77 Sing this song about worship to the tune, *We Wish You a Merry Christmas*.

Wherever people gather, (3x)
  Sweep right arm outward
To worship the Lord,
  Sweep both arms upward
He said that He would join them, (3x)
  Right arm up, then sweep outward
He's a risen, living Lord.
  Down on one knee, then stand with arms upward

78 This song, to the tune of *There's a Hole in the Bottom of the Sea*, progresses from a short song to a long song by adding a new line which is sung two times for each verse. The actions are written only the first time a line appears, but repeat the action every time that line appears. Here's how to sing it the first time through:

There is room in the Sunday school for you.
  Clap in rhythm
There is room in the Sunday school for you.
There is room
  Swing right arm out
There is room
  Swing left arm out
There is room in the Sunday school for you.

Here's the second verse:
Won't you please take a seat?
  Sit down
For there's room in the Sunday school for you.
  Stand and clap in rhythm
Won't you please take a seat?
For there's room in the Sunday school for you.
There is room, there is room
There is room in the Sunday school for you.

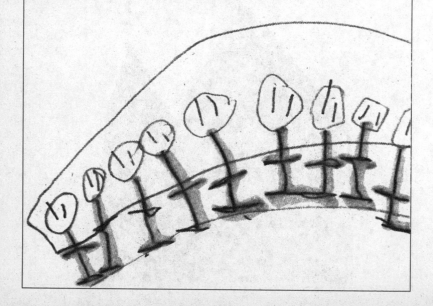

Here's the last (seventh verse):
It just can't be beat!
    Stomp feet
Knowing Jesus is a treat.
    Snap fingers
Bible stories are neat.
    Slap thighs
There are new friends to meet.
    Shake hands with person next to you
There's a teacher to greet.
    Wave hello to teacher
Won't you please take a seat
    Sit down
For there's room in the Sunday school for you.
It just can't be beat!
Knowing Jesus is a treat.
Bible stories are neat.
There are new friends to meet.
There's a teacher to greet.
Won't you please take a seat
For there's room in the Sunday school for you.
There is room, there is room
There is room in the Sunday school for you.

79 *Buffalo Gals* is the tune for this fun song about getting ready for Sunday school. Clap in rhythm on the last line of every verse.

Boys and girls, time to get up today,
    Squat down; jump up every time you sing "get up"
Get up today, get up today.
Boys and girls, time to get up today.
It's time for Sunday school.

Find your shoes and put on your clothes,
    Pretend to dress
Put on your clothes, put on your clothes,
Find your shoes and put on your clothes,
It's time for Sunday school.

Get your Bible and offering,
    Pretend to hold Bible; put offering in pocket or purse
Offering, offering.
Get your Bible and offering.
It's time for Sunday school.

Hurry up, kids! Now don't be late.
    Run in place
Don't be late, don't be late.
Hurry up, kids! Now don't be late.
It's time for Sunday school.

Climb in the car and fasten the belt,
    Act out these words
Fasten the belt, fasten the belt.
Climb in the car and fasten the belt.
It's time for Sunday school.

Here we are. Now, go to church.
    Walk in place
Go to church, go to church.
Here we are. Now, go to church.
It's time for Sunday school.

80
Sing these words about going to church to the tune of *This Is My Father's World*.

Wh~y do we come to church?
Sing this verse with hands on hips
Wh~y do we praise God's name?
Why do we gather here each week?
Why are we glad we came?
We come because we know
Point to self, then to head
That our God does love us so.
Point up, then cross hands over heart
Through Jesus Christ, we can have new life.
Sweep left arm out, then right arm
He paid the debt we owe.
Sweep both arms upward

81
Sing these words to the tune of *Go In and Out the Window* or *Farmer in the Dell*. Clap on the the last line of each verse.

Let's worship God together. (3x)
Arms at side, then sweep them upward
And off'rings gladly bring.

Let's tell Him that we're thankful. (3x)
Cup hands around mouth, then sweep them upward
And joyful praises sing.

Let's show Him that we love Him. (3x)
Nod head and pat shoulder of person next to you
He gave us everything.

Let's tell the world about Him. (3x)
Skip in place
For He's our heav'nly King.

Christmas Songs

82 Sing this action rhyme to the familiar Christmas carol, *O Come, All Ye Faithful.*

The angels are singing.
Point to mouth, then sweep hands outward
The shepherds quickly running.
Run in place
A new star is shining over Bethlehem bright.
Put hand overhead and wiggle fingers
Mary is smiling, smiling on sweet Jesus.
Smile and pretend to rock baby
Sweet Jesus is sleeping.
Rest head on hands
Sweet Jesus is sleeping.
Put finger to lips as if saying sh-h-h
Sweet Jesus is sleeping
Rest head on hands
This holy night.
Stretch arms outward

83 Sing this action song, "Jesus Christ Is Born," to the tune of *Clap, Clap, Clap Your Hands.* If that tune is not familiar, adapt the words to fit *Skip to My Lou.* Have children act out the verses as a mini-play. Select volunteers to be Mary, Joseph, and the other characters.

Refrain:
Clap, clap, clap your hands.
   Clap in rhythm
Jesus Christ is born.
   Raise arms upward, then extend them outward
Clap, clap, clap your hands.
Jesus Christ is born.

His mother Mary is standing by,
Standing by the manger.
Kindly Joseph's keeping watch
And welcoming the strangers.
Repeat refrain

The angels told the shepherd boys
Of His holy birth.
They hurried off to Bethlehem
With praise and joyous mirth.
Repeat refrain

The wisemen traveled from the East.
They journeyed from afar.
They kept their eyes turned up to heaven
And followed Jesus' star.
Repeat refrain

84

The familiar tune, *Old MacDonald*, works well for this rhyme about Jesus' birth.

"Baby Jesus will be born."
  Cup hands around mouth
Clap your hands with me.
  Clap in rhythm
Mary heard the angel tell.
  Cup hand behind ear
Clap them joyfully. (Clap)
Clap your hands—1, 2, 3
  Stomp feet on each number
Clap your hands so joyfully. (Clap)
"Baby Jesus will be born."
Clap your hands with me. (Clap)

Joseph heard it in a dream.
  Rest head on hands
Clap your hands with me. (Clap)
God plans all things very well.
  Point upward; then sweep arm from left to right
Clap them joyfully. (Clap)
Clap your hands—1, 2, 3
Clap your hands so joyfully. (Clap)
"Baby Jesus will be born."
Clap your hands with me. (Clap)

85

Sing the tune for the chorus of *Jingle Bells* for this rhyme about Jesus' birth.

Shepherds lay in a field,
Lean chin on one hand; put other hand on hip
Watching sheep at night.
Suddenly, an angel choir
Quickly, get in an "I'm frightened" position
Gave them all a fright!
"Please don't fear.
Extend arms, palms outward, shaking head
God sent us here.
Point upward
Good News we have to share.
Cup hands around mouth
Hurry off to Bethlehem!
Run in place
You'll find the Christ Child there."
Bend on one knee; extend arms with palms upward

86

These words fit easily to tune of the Christmas song, *O Christmas Tree.*

O Christmas star, O Christmas star.
Stretch arms out in front
Shine on the earth so brightly.
Make circle with arms overhead
O Christmas star, O Christmas star.
Shine on the earth so brightly.
The Wise Men come from far away.
Walk in place
Light their paths so they won't stray,
Shield eyes with hands
And guide them unto Bethlehem,
Where Jesus lies a-sleeping.
Rest head on hands

87 Have fun singing this to *Deck the Halls*. Use bells and tambourines every time children sing "fa-la-la-la." Have them shake their instruments overhead.

Children 'round the world are singing,
Fa la la la la, la la la la.
Praises to the Lord they're bringing
Fa la la la la, la la la la.
In the air of every nation,
Fa la la la la, la la la la,
Are the sounds of celebration,
Fa la la la la, la la la la.

88 Sing these words to the fun holiday tune, *We Wish You a Merry Christmas*.

We bring you Good News at Christmas. (3x)
  Sweep right arm outward, then left
Christ Jesus is born.
  Clap in rhythm

In swaddling cloth they wrapped Him. (3x)
  Stand with arms folded across chest
To keep the Babe warm.
  Pretend to rock baby

The shepherds all came to worship. (3x)
  Kneel with head bowed
That first Christmas morn.
  Raise arms upward

89 These words about the joys of Christmas can be sung to *When Johnny Comes Marching Home.* Let children use their imaginations to think of actions. You might ask five volunteers to each take a verse to act out while the rest of the children sing the words.

Chrístmas is a cóming,
And I'm hélping decoráte.
There's lóts of gifts to búy and wrap;
Sweet cóokies to be báked.
We'll róll the dough really níce and thin
And cárefully cut out the shápes.
Then we'll báke-them in-the oven for
Jésus Christ's birthdáy.

I'm ín the Christmas prógram,
And I háve a song to síng.
The prógram will tell éveryone
Abóut the newborn Kíng.
God sént Him down to-earth fróm above
As júst a tiny-wee, líttle babe.
Mary fíxed a mánger-bed for
Jésus Christ's birthdáy.

I wánt to open all my présents;
I can hardly wait.
But thére's another réason why
I wánt to celebráte.
The Bíble tells me that Jésus came
To téll us all about Gód's great love.
I'm so véry háppy! It's
Jésus Christ's birthdáy.

What tréasure can I gíve to Jesus?
Whát gift can I bríng?
I cán't afford a fáncy jewel
Or shíny golden ríng.
My móther says that the ónly thing
That Jésus wa~ants is *me*.
So I'm wrápping-all-the lóve-I-have for
Jésus Christ's birthdáy.

90 As children sing this action rhyme to *Skip to My Lou*, have them step on their right foot and clap to the right; then step on the left and clap left in rhythm, like this: 1-right step, 2-right clap, 3-left step, 4-left clap. Repeat the song, singing it a little faster each time.

The shepherds heard the angels say
"A Savior's born for you today!"
And I just want to say it's true,
That Jesus came to save you, too!

91 Sing this Christmas song called "The Best Christmas Gift" to the familiar Sunday school tune, *The Wiseman Built His House Upon a Rock*. Let children select a different action to do in rhythm for each verse, such as swaying from side to side or bending knees up and down.

The véry best Christmas gift of them all
Wásn't a sled or a bike or a doll.
The véry best Christmas gift instead
Láy on a manger bed.

On-a mánger bed in a stable lay
Gód's own Son just born that day.
With Máry and Joseph sitting by,
A bríght star shone on high.

The shépherds came to worship the King.
And wísemen gifts of treasure did bring.
And ángels' songs were sung on earth
To téll of Jesus' birth.

Repeat first verse

92

Sing this action song about the Christmas story to *Jimmy Crack Corn.*

Joseph smiled at God's own Son. (3x)
Bend knees on each beat
In the stable brightly.
Smile really big

Mary rocked Him in her arms. (3x)
Sway back and forth in rhythm
While cows said "moo" so quietly.
Say "moo" *very* quietly

Clap your hands now 1, 2, 3! (3x)
Slap thighs on each beat; but clap hands on numbers
And welcome Jesus with me.
Extend arms outward

93

Use the tune, *Over the River and Through the Woods,* to sing this rhyme.

People give gifts to the ones they love.
Sweep right arm outward, then left arm outward
But what can we give God—
Shrug shoulders
A mountain tall, a flower small?
Form peak with hands overhead; then squat down
The Lord God made them all.
Point upward
What could He need? Oh, what could He want
Shrug right shoulder, then left
That we could ever give?
Point to self, then extend hands with palms upward
I know! Let's give Him all our love,
Snap fingers, then cross hands over heart
And always for Him we'll live.
Raise arms upward

94 Use *Swing Low, Sweet Chariot* to sing this Christmas praise. When children sing, "Praise You! Praise You, God!" have them raise right arms, then left, and, finally, kneel as they say "God." Let them determine actions for the rest of the song.

Refrain:
A babe is born tonight.
Praise You! Praise You, God!
The angels sing with pure delight!
Praise You! Praise You, God!

The King of Creation
Is bringing salvation.
Praise You! Praise You, God!
With shepherds a kneelin'
God's people are a feelin'
Great joy! Praise You, God!

Refrain:
The stars join in the song.
Praise You! Praise You, God!
The sun and moon—they hum along.
Praise You! Praise You, God!

A new star's a blazin'.
It's truly amazin'.
Praise You! Praise You, God!
All of creation's
Announcin' to the nations
Praise You! Praise You, God!

Refrain:
We're clappin' and we're laughin'.
Praise You! Praise You, God!
The mountains ringin'; the whole world singin'.
Praise You! Praise You, God!

Don't hesitate
To help celebrate.
Praise You! Praise You, God!
It gives God joy for
Each girl and boy to
Praise You! Praise You, God!

95 Have children sing this Christmas rhyme to the tune, *Eensy Weensy Spider*. Have children keep the beat for this rhyme by snapping their fingers or shifting their weight from right foot to left foot.

He díd it. He díd it.
Our Gód did what He sáid.
Our Kíng came all ríght,
But He's wrínkled and He's réd.
Why dón't you belíeve me?
Why dó you say maybé?
I thínk it's quite cléver;
He cáme as a baby.

A báby, a báby!
Gód's this baby's dád.
Máry will raíse Him
While Hé is still a lád.
Jóseph will teách Him
To bé a carpentér.
And Jésus will grów up
To bé our Savіór.

A prómise, a prómise!
Oh, whát God says is trúe.
Sátan can't cónquer
When Jésus' helping yóu.
Wíth sins forgíven
We'll stánd before God's thróne.
A prómise, a prómise!
That héaven will be our hóme.

Easter Songs

96 Sing this song called "Jesus Is Alive" to the tune of *Camptown Races*.

Easter flowers are blooming bright.
　Put wrists together, spreading fingers apart
Jesus is-ali~ive!
　Squat down; then jump up with arms upward
Hear the church bells sound the news,
　Put hands together and swing arms back and forth
Jesus Christ's alive.
　Squat down; then jump up with arms upward
Go and tell the world.
　Sweep arms outward
Shout aloud the news.
　Cup hands around mouth
Jesus Christ has risen!
　Point up
And He's still alive!
　Squat down; then jump up with arms upward

97 Have children clap in rhythm as they skip around the room singing these words to *Skip to My Lou*. Or, have the children use rhythm instruments as they sing. Some kids might enjoy writing more verses.

Everybody clap and sing. (3x)
The stone is rolled away.

Jesus is alive and He (3x)
Is with us every day!

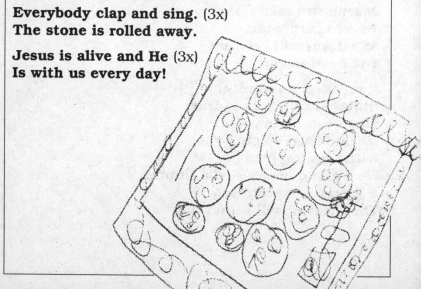

98

The Easter story from Matthew 28:1-7 can be acted out as a mini-play. Challenge kids to come up actions to tell the story as they sing this to the tune of *Yankee Doodle*.

Mary and the other Mary
Rose at dawn on Sunday.
They went to loo~ook at the tomb
But the stone was rolled away.
Refrain:
He is risen; He's alive.
Jesus lives forever!
Let's go spread the news that He
Is rís'n and lives forever.

There was a very big earthquake,
The stone rolled from the door.
An angel came and said to them.
"Jesus is there no more."
Refrain

The angel said to both Marys,
"Oh, please, now don't you fear.
Jesús' is ris'n just as He said.
He's-alíve. He is not hére."
Refrain

"Spread the news; tell His disciples,
Now be on your way."
The Marys ran to spread the news.
"This is a wonderful day!"
Refrain

99 Sing this happy action song of praise to *Camptown Races.* Every time children sing "Jesus rose up from the dead," have them put their right foot in front of the left and rock back and forth on each beat.

Jesus rose up from the dead.
Glory, glory!
　Raise arms each time you sing "glory"
Jesus rose up from the dead.
Glory to His name! (2x)
　Raise arms on "glory"; then clap after singing "name"
Shout this glad refrain.
　Cup hands around mouth
Jesus rose up from the dead.
Glory to His name!

100 This song, "Good Friday Song," is to the familiar Sunday school tune, *I Will Make You Fisher's of Men.* These words have an important message for all of us. Discuss the meaning of the verses with the children.

Why do we call Good Friday good,
　Use fingers to push up mouth into smile
Good Friday good, good Friday good?
Why do we call Good Friday good
When it seems so sad?
　Use fingers to pull mouth down into frown
Isn't dying bad?
Shouldn't we feel sad?
Why do we call Good Friday good,
　Use fingers to push up mouth into smile
When it seems so sad?
　Use fingers to pull mouth down into frown

Jesus died. Oh, yes, that is true.
　Hold arms to the sides, shoulder height
Yes, that is true, yes, that is true.
Jesus died. Oh, yes, that is true,
But it isn't bad.
　Use fingers to push up mouth into smile
Even though it's sad,

Use fingers to pull mouth down into frown

Jesus' death's not bad.

Jesus died. Oh, yes, that is true,

Hold arms to the sides, shoulder height

But it isn't bad.

Use fingers to push up mouth into smile

By Christ's death we can be set free,

Sweep arms upward

Can be set free, can be set free.

By Christ's death we can be set free,

Free from Satan's power.

Fold arms tightly across chest

In that sad, dark hour

Jesus broke sin's power.

Thrust arms downward

By Christ's death we can be set free,

Sweep arms upward

Free from Satan's power.

Do you see why Good Friday's good,

Use fingers to push up mouth into smile

Good Friday's good, good Friday's good?

Do you see why Good Friday's good

Even though it's sad?

Use fingers to pull mouth down into frown

Things that seem so sad

Are not always bad.

When Christ died, He rose from the grave.

We're no longer sad.

Use fingers to push up mouth into smile